ESSENTIAL ALBANIAN GRAMMAR

Emsal Karar

ESSENTIAL ALBANIAN GRAMMAR

OPPIAN

Oppian Press
Helsinki, 2024
ISBN 978-952-83-0016-8

TABLE OF CONTENTS

INTRODUCTION

Welcome to Essential Albanian Grammar! This concise yet comprehensive guide is the perfect resource for anyone looking to learn the fundamentals of the Albanian language, which has a rich and fascinating history.

Albanian is an Indo-European language spoken by approximately 7-8 million people, primarily in Albania, Kosovo, North Macedonia, and in Albanian diaspora communities around the world. It is the only extant language in its branch of the Indo-European family tree.

The origins of Albanian language are still debated among linguists. One prominent theory is that Albanian descended from the ancient Illyrian languages spoken in the western Balkans in antiquity. However, the lack of written records prior to the 15th century makes it difficult to establish a definitive link. Other hypotheses propose that Albanian originated from Thracian, Dacian, or another Paleo-Balkan language.

Regardless of its precise origins, Albanian has been shaped by its contact with various languages over the centuries. From the 2nd century BC to the 5th century AD, Albanian absorbed vocabulary from Greek and Latin. Later influences came from Slavic languages, Germanic languages (through migrations), and Turkish during the Ottoman period.

The earliest surviving documents in Albanian date back to the 15th century. However, a standardized orthography using the Latin alphabet was not adopted until 1909. Prior to that, Albanian was written using a mix of alphabets and spelling conventions.

Today, there are two main dialects of Albanian: Gheg in the north (including Kosovo and Macedonia) and Tosk in the south. Standard Albanian is based more on the Tosk dialect.

In this book, we'll take you step-by-step through the core elements of Albanian grammar, including:

- Nouns – their gender, number, definiteness, and declension patterns.
- Pronouns – personal pronouns, possessive pronouns, and the unique clitic forms.
- Adjectives – their agreement with nouns, position, and comparative forms.
- Verbs – key verbs, person, number, voice, mood, tenses, and conjugation.
- Word Order – the typical sentence structures used in Albanian.

By the end, you'll have a solid foundation in how the Albanian language works grammatically. The chapters are build logically, with plenty of examples to illustrate each point.

Albanian grammar does have some unique features compared to other Indo-European languages. But this book makes the concepts approachable for language learners, focusing on the essential structures needed to start using the language.

We hope Essential Albanian Grammar will be a helpful companion on your language learning journey, giving you an appreciation for the Albanian language's intriguing history while enabling you to progress quickly in your mastery of how it works. Gëzuar! (Enjoy!)

NOUNS

In Albanian, nouns reflect the grammatical categories of gender, number and case. Another significant classification of Albanian nouns is also the distinction between definiteness and indefiniteness.

Definiteness and Indefiniteness

Nouns in Albanian have two distinct forms: the indefinite and the definite. The indefinite articles "a" and "an" are equivalent to "një" in Albanian. Yet, indefinite nouns are not always preceded by "një"; they can be used alone. There are no equivalents for definite articles in Albanian. Instead, definite nouns take different endings.

> Indefinite nouns: vend (place), shok (friend), rrugë (street)
> Definite nouns: vend**i** (the place) shok**u** (the friend) rrug**a** (the street)

How to know which form to use?

The indefinite nouns "vend", "shok", "rrugë" refer to a place, friend or street in general. They can name a place, friend or street that was unknown until then and is being mentioned for the first time: Erdhi një shok (A friend came) does not specify who that friend is.

The definite nouns "vendi", "shoku", "rruga" mark a specific place, friend or street that can be distinguished from the others. Shihemi te vendi i zakonshëm (Let's meet at our usual place).

Definite nouns are used when it is clear from the context what the noun refers to: Shoku ynë erdhi (Our friend came); it is known who the friend is.

Gender

All nouns in Albanian have the category of gender. There are three genders: masculine, feminine and neuter. The majority of nouns are either masculine or feminine, and only a minority are neuter.

The gender of the nouns is distinguished through word endings:

a) The noun is masculine if it ends in a consonant in its indefinite form, and then in the definite form takes the ending **-i** or **-u**.

        Indefinite   Definite

        tre**n** (train) – tren - **i** - (the train)
        zo**g** (bird) – zog - **u** - (the bird)

b) Some nouns are masculine if they end in a vowel in indefinite form and in the definite form take the ending **-ri.**

        Indefinite   Definite

        dr**u** (wood) – dru**ri** (the wood)
        p**e** (thread) – pe**ri** (the thread)

c) Some nouns are masculine if in their indefinite form they end in the stressed vowels:

-i, -a, -e.

        Indefinite   Definite

        sh**i** (rain) – shi**u** (the rain)
        bab**a** (father) – baba**i** (the father)
        atdh**e** (motherland) – atdhe**u** (the motherland)

a) The noun is feminine if in its indefinite form it ends with **-ë** or **-e,** whereas in definite form it ends with **-a,** or **-ja**.

Indefinite	Definite
Der**ë** (door)	der**a** (the door)
Lul**e** (flower)	lul**ja** (the flower)

Note: Perceive how in the examples above, in the definite form of the noun, -ë and -e drop and change into -a and -ja correspondingly.

Nouns with these endings are typically feminine. Some exceptions are: burrë, djalë, gjumë, djathë, ujë, mjaltë. Even though they end with -ë in their indefinite form, they are masculine because in their definite form they take the ending -i: burr-i, djal-i, gjum-i, djath-i, uj-i, mjalt-i.

b) The noun is feminine if it ends in the consonants **-l, ll, m, n, r, rr,** which are preceded by an unstressed **ë** or **u** and in the definite form they still take the endings **-a**:

       veg**ël** (tool) – veg**la** (the tool)

       vet**ull** (eyebrow) – vetull**a** (the eyebrow)

       zem**ër** (heart) – zemr**a** (the heart)

       ënd**ërr** (dream) – ëndrr**a** (the dream)

*Note how the **ë** drops in definite form.*

There are a few exceptions: dim**ër** (winter) – dim**ri** (the winter), av**ull** (vapor) – avull**i** (the vapor), pluh**ur** (dust) – pluhur**i** (the dust). They are masculine because in the definite form, they take the ending **-i**.

c) Some nouns are feminine if they end in **-a, -e, -o** and in definite form take the ending **-ja:**

Kal**a** (tower) – kala**ja** (the tower)
Radi**o** (radio) – radio**ja** (the radio)
Nus**e** (bride) – nus**ja** (the bride)

d) Nouns that end in **-ëri** or **-ësi** in indefinite form are feminine. In the definite form, as usual, they take the ending **-a:**

drejt**ësi** (justice) – drejtësi**a** (the justice)
trim**ëri** (bravery) – trimëri**a** (the bravery)

a) The noun is neuter if in its definite form it ends in **-t**, **-it** or **-ët**:

Të folur – të folur**it** (speaking)
Të ftohtë – të ftoht**ët** (coldness)

Ambigender

In Albanian, most nouns maintain the same gender for both singular and plural forms. Yet, one intriguing characteristic of the language is that certain nouns, more specifically the masculine nouns that in plural take the **-e** or **-ra** endings in indefinite form and **-et** or **-rat** in definite form, are converted into feminine gender:

Deti i pafund (the endless sea) – Det**et** e pafunda (the endless seas)
Fshati i gjerë (this large village) – Fshat**rat** e gjera (the large villages)

In the examples above, "deti" and "fshati" are masculine; the masculine adjectives "i pafund" and "i gjerë" are used accordingly. In plural, these nouns take the endings **-et** and **-rat** respectively, and become feminine. The change can be noted by the use of the feminine form of the adjectives "e pafunda", "e gjera" to refer to the plural nouns. This phenomenon is known as "dygjinishmëri" or "ambigender", and is quite common in contemporary Albanian language.

Changing the gender of a noun

In Albanian, in some cases, different words are used to refer to people of different genders. For example:

> nënë (mother) – baba (father)
> grua (woman) – burrë (man)
> pulë (chicken) – gjel (rooster)

Generally, the feminine form of the noun derives from the masculine. One can typically change the gender of the noun from masculine to feminine by adding suffixes:

> **Suffix -e:** mik (friend/masculine) – mik**e** (friend/feminine), gjysh (grandfather) – gjysh**e** (grandmother);
> Suffix **-ë:** plak (old man) – plak**ë** (old woman);
> Suffix **-eshë:** perëndi (God) – perënd**eshë** (Goddess), drejtor (director) – drejtor**eshë** (directress); luan (lion) – luan**eshë** (lioness)
> Suffix **-ushë**: dren (deer) – dren**ushë** (doe), ari (bear) – ar**ushë** (sow)
> Suffix: **onjë** -ujk (he wolf) – ujk**onjë** (she wolf)

Number

In Albanian, nouns have two numbers: singular and plural. The plural is usually formed by adding suffixes to the singular nouns. However, in certain cases, apart from suffixes, there are also some phonological changes.

Forming the plural of masculine nouns

Most nouns form the plural by taking certain endings:

a) **-e** – qytet (city) – qytet**e** (cities); hotel (hotel) – hotel**e** (hotels)
   Reminder: The masculine nouns that take this ending in plural change the gender and become feminine.

b) **-ë** – punëtor (worker) – punëtor**ë** (workers); shok (friend) – shok**ë** (friends)

c) **-a** – pëllumb (dove) – pëllumb**a** (doves); telefon (phone) – telefon**a** (phones)

d) **-enj** – lumë (river) – lum**enj** (rivers); budalla (fool) – budall**enj** (fools)

e) **-nj** -dru (wood)- dru**nj** (woods); hero (hero) – hero**nj** (heroes)

f) **-inj** – shkop (stick) – shkop**inj** (sticks), shkëmb (rock) – shkëmb**inj** (rocks)

g) **-ër** -mbret (king) – mbret**ër** (kings), prind (parent) -prind**ër** (parents)

h) **-ra** – lojë (game) – lojë**ra** (games), fshat (village) – fshat**ra** (villages)
   Reminder: The masculine nouns that take this ending in plural change the gender and become feminine.

i) Some nouns remain the same in plural: një nxënës (one student) – disa nxënës (several students), një shitës (one seller) – disa shitës (several sellers), një mësues (one teacher) – disa mësues (several teachers)

The plural of some masculine nouns is formed simply by changing the vowels or constants:

a) -a changes to -e – d**a**sh – d**e**sh

b) -k changes to -q – armi**k** (enemy) -armi**q** (enemies); uj**k** (wolf) -uj**q** (wolves)

c) -g changes to -gj – zo**g** (bird) – zo**gj** (birds)

d) -ll changes to -j – portoka**ll** (orange) – portoka**j** (oranges); sheku**ll** (century) -sheku**j** (centuries)

e) -r changes to -j – bi**r** (son) -bi**j** (sons); lepu**r** (rabbit) – lepu**j** (rabbits)

Finally, some masculine nouns, in order to form the plural, change the vowel or consonant AND add an ending:

a) -k changes to q plus -e – shka**k** (cause)- shka**q-e** (causes)

b) -g changes to -gj plus – e – lën**g** (juice) – lën**gj-e** (juices)

c) -a changes to -e plus k changes to q – pl**ak** (old man) -pl**eq** (old men)

Note: All the plurals above are in indefinite form. In definite form they either take -t or -të such as shokët, zogjtë, etc.

Forming the plural of feminine nouns

To form the plural, feminine nouns either take the ending **-a,** or **-ra** or remain the same.

a) **-a** -nënë (mother) – nën**a** (mothers); flutur (butterfly)– flutur**a** (butterflies)

b) **-ra**- verë (wine) – ver**ëra** (wines); gjë (thing) – gj**ëra** (things)

c) They remain the same: një ditë (one day) – disa ditë (several days), një rrugë (one street) – disa rrugë (several streets), një mollë (one apple) – disa mollë (several apples), një shtëpi (one house) – disa shtëpi (several houses), një re (one cloud) – re (several clouds)

Note: All the plurals above are in indefinite form. In definite form they either take -t or -të such as nënat, fluturat, ditët, mollët, shtëpitë, retë.

Declension

There are three types of declension:

a) 1st declension: Masculine nouns ending in -i in definite form: mal-i (the mountain), det-i (the sea), qiell-i (the sky)

b) 2nd declension: Masculine nouns ending in -u in definite form: zog-u (the bird), breg-u (the shore), mik-u (the friend)

c) 3rd declension: Feminine nouns ending in -a or -ja in definite form: hën-a (the moon), nën-a (the mother), rrufe-ja (the thunder)

In some Albanian grammar books, a fourth type of declension is also included for neuter nouns which end in -t or -të - të ngrënët (eating)

Since the noun can have various syntactic functions within a sentence such as subject, complement, determiner, direct or indirect object, depending on the function, the noun will take a specific case form with a specific ending accordingly. The changing of endings when used in different cases is known as declension.

In contemporary Albanian, there are five cases:

1. Nominative (Emërore): The noun in the nominative case usually functions as a Subject.
2. Genitive/Possessive (Gjinore): The noun plays the role of a Determiner or a Subject Complement.
3. Dative (Dhanore): The noun functions as Indirect Object without preposition.
4. Accusative (Kallëzore): The noun mainly functions as Direct Object.
5. Ablative (Rrjedhore): The noun functions as Indirect Object with preposition.

All Albanian nouns are declined in these cases. Since Albanian nouns have indefinite and definite form, there is also indefinite and definite declension as well as singular and plural declension.

INDEFINITE NOUNS DECLENSION

Libër (book)	Shok (friend)	Ditë (day)

Singular

Singular

Singular

Libër	Shok	Ditë
(Nom) libër	(Nom) shok	(Nom) ditë
(Gen) i/e/të/së (një) libri	(Gen) i/e/të/së (një) shoku	(Gen) i/e/të/së (një) dite
(Dat) (një) libri	(Dat) (një) shoku	(Dat) (një) dite
(Acc) (një) libër	(Acc) (një) shok	(Acc) (një) ditë
(Abl) (një) libri	(Abl) (një) shoku	(Abl) (një) dite

Plural

Plural

Plural

Plural	Plural	Plural
(Nom) libra	(Nom) shokë	(Nom) ditë
(Gen i/e/të/së (disa) librave	(Gen) i/e/të/së (disa) shokëve	(Gen) i/e/të/së (disa) ditëve
(Dat) (disa) librave	(Dat) (disa) shokëve	(Dat) (disa) ditëve
(Acc) (disa) libra	(Acc) (disa) shokë	(Acc) (disa) ditë
(Abl) (disa) librash	(Abl) (disa) shokësh	(Abl) (disa) ditësh

DEFINITE NOUNS DECLENSION

libri (1st declension)	shoku (2nd declension)	dita (3rd declension)
(The book)	(The friend)	(The day)

Singular	**Singular**	**Singular**
(Nom) Libri	(Nom) shoku	(Nom) dita
(Gen) i/e/të/së librit	(Gen) i/e/të/së shokut	(Gen) i/e/të/së ditës
(Dat) librit	(Dat) shokut	(Dat) ditës
(Acc) librin	(Acc) shokun	(Acc) ditën
(Abl) librit	(Abl) shokut	(Abl) ditës

Plural	**Plural**	**Plural**
(Nom) librat	(Nom) shokët	(Nom) ditët
(Gen) i/e/të/së librave	(Gen) i/e/të/së shokëve	(Gen) i/e/të/së ditëve
(Dat) librave	(Dat) shokëve	(Dat) ditëve
(Acc) librat	(Acc) shokët	(Acc) ditët
(Abl) (prej) librave	(Abl) shokëve	(Abl) ditëve

Note: *In plural, all nouns are declined in the same way, that is, they take the same endings, no matter which declension they are in, 1st, 2nd or 3rd.*

The Genitive case of the noun is analogous to the English possessive case; it indicates possessiveness: libri i Benit – Ben's book. It can also indicate type: pema e mollës (apple tree) or place: mali i Pashtrikut (Pashtrik's mountain).

A noun in the genitive case, apart from the specific ending it takes, is also accompanied by an article that precedes it: i, e, të, së. The type of the article that accompanies the noun in genitive case is determined by the gender, number and case of the noun that precedes the noun in genitive case: libri **i** Borës (singular masculine noun), shtëpia **e** Borës (singular feminine noun), shtëpisë **së** Borës (noun "shtëpisë" in dative case), librave **të** Borës (noun in plural).

PERSONAL PRONOUNS

Personal pronouns in Albanian are as follows:

Singular	*Plural*
Unë – I	Ne – we
Ti – You	Ju - you
Ai – He	Ata – they (masculine)
Ajo – She	Ato – they (feminine)

In Albanian, the third person makes a distinction in gender both in singular and plural, using different forms for feminine and masculine: ai, ata (masculine) and ajo, ato (feminine).
If the gender of the third person is not known by the speaker, the expression "ai ose ajo" (he or she) is used. Similarly, if the gender in third person plural is not known, one can say "ata ose ato". Additionally, in third person plural, when referring to a pair or a group of people, animals, objects or any other entities that consist of both genders, feminine and masculine, then the plural masculine pronoun "ata" is used, which encompasses both genders.

The plural second person pronoun, "ju", apart from denoting two or more people being addressed, can also be used to address someone in singular. It is a matter of courtesy and a sign of respect to refer to a single person with the plural second person pronoun "ju":

Më falni zonjë, **ju** po më kërkonit? – Excuse me madam, were you looking for me?

Declension

Personal pronouns reflect the category of case.

They take different forms when used in different cases:

Nominative	Unë	Ti	Ai	Ajo	Ne	Ju	Ata	Ato
Genitive	/	/	i/e/të/së atij	i/e/të/së asaj	/	/	i/e/të/së atyre	i/e/të/së atyre
Dative	mua, më	ty, të	atij, i	asaj, i	neve, na	juve, ju	atyre, u	atyre, u
Accusative	mua, më	ty, të	atë, e	atë, e	ne, na	ju, ju	ata, i	ato, u
Abblative	meje	teje	atij	asaj	nesh	jush	atyre	atyre

When used in different functions, personal pronouns take different forms:

Unë e pashë shefin. (I saw the boss) – "Unë" (Nominative) acting as Subject
Shefi më pa **mua.**   (The boss saw me) – "mua" (Accusative) acting as Direct Object.

First and second person singular and plural do not reflect the genitive case.

The personal pronouns can be dropped when the subject of the verb is clear:

Unë fola. – Fola. (I spoke.)
Ne u ulëm. – U ulëm. (We sat down.)
Ai mbërriti. – Mbërriti. (He arrived)

The abbreviated forms of personal pronouns

In the dative and accusative case, personal pronouns also have abbreviated forms:
më, të, e, na, ju, i, u. They can be used in sentences with or without the full form
of the pronoun.

    a)   Ty të tha të shkoje me të.

                                (He told you to go with him.)

    b)   Të tha të shkoje me të.

    a)   Juve ju treguan për ndodhinë.

                                  (They told you about the occurrence).

    b)   Ju treguan për ndodhinë.

    a)   Atyre u dhanë shumë dhurata.

                                  (They have them a lot of presents.)

    b)   U dhanë shumë dhurata.

POSSESSIVE PRONOUNS

Possessive pronouns in Albanian are either accompanied by nouns or used alone. They agree with the noun in terms of person, number and gender.

Possessive pronouns used with nouns:

1st person singular: im, ime, e mi, të mia

   a)   im is used with singular masculine noun - Libri **im** (my book)
   b)   ime is used with singular feminine noun -   Shtëpia **ime** (my house)
   c)   e mi is used with plural masculine noun - Librat **e mi** (my books)
   d)   e mia is used with plural feminine noun – Shtëpitë **e mia** (my houses)

2nd person singular: yt, jote, e tu, e tua

   a)   yt is used with singular masculine noun – libri **yt** (your book)
   b)   jote is used with singular feminine noun – Shtëpia **jote** (your house)
   c)   e tu is used with plural masculine noun – librat **e tu** (your books)
   d)   e tua is used with plural feminine noun – Shtëpitë **e tua** (your houses)

3rd person singular (masculine): i tij, e tij

   a)   i tij is used with singular masculine noun – libri **i tij** (his book)
   b)   e tij is used with singular feminine noun – Shtëpia **e tij** (his house)
   c)   e tij is used with plural masculine noun – librat **e tij** (his books)
   d)   e tij is used with plural feminine noun – Shtëpitë **e tij** (his houses)

3rd person singular (feminine): i saj, e saj

    a)   i saj is used with singular masculine noun – libri **i saj** (her book)
    b)   e saj is used with singular feminine noun – Shtëpia **e saj** (her house)
    c)   e saj is used with plural masculine noun – librat **e saj** (her books)
    d)   e saj is used with plural feminine noun – Shtëpitë **e saj** (her houses)

1st person plural: ynë, jonë, tanë, tona

    a)   ynë is used with singular masculine noun – libri **ynë** (our book)
    b)   jonë is used with singular feminine noun – Shtëpia **jonë** (our house)
    c)   tanë is used with plural masculine noun – librat **tanë** (our books)
    d)   tona is used with plural feminine noun – Shtëpitë **tona** (our houses)

2nd person plural: juaj, tuaj

    a)   juaj is used with singular masculine noun – libri **juaj** (your book)
    b)   juaj is used with singular feminine noun – Shtëpia **juaj** (your house)
    c)   tuaj is used with plural masculine noun – librat **tuaj** (your books)
    d)   tuaja is used with plural feminine noun – Shtëpitë **tuaja** (your houses)

3rd person singular (both masculine and feminine): i tyre, e tyre

    a)   i tyre is used with singular masculine noun – libri **i tyre** (their book)
    b)   e tyre is used with singular feminine noun – Shtëpia **e tyre** (their house)
    c)   e tyre is used with plural masculine noun – librat **e tyre** (their books)
    d)   e tyre is used with plural feminine noun – Shtëpitë **e tyre** (their houses)

Possessive pronouns used alone:

1ˢᵗ person singular: imi, imja, të mitë, të miat

- a) imi is used with singular masculine noun – Libri është **imi**.
  (The book is mine.)
- b) imja is used with singular feminine noun – Shtëpia është **imja.**
  (The house is mine.)
- c) të mitë is used with plural masculine noun – Librat janë **të mitë.**
  (The books are mine.)
- d) të miat is used with plural feminine noun Shtëpitë janë **të miat.**
  (The houses are mine.)

2ⁿᵈ person singular: yti, jotja, të tutë, të tuat

- a) I yti is used with singular masculine noun - Libri është **yti**.
  (The book is yours).
- b) e jotja is used with singular feminine noun – Shtëpia është **jotja.**
  (The house is yours.)
- c) të tutë is used with plural masculine noun – Librat janë **të tutë.**
  (The books are yours)
- d) të tuat is used with plural feminine noun - Shtëpitë janë **të tuat.**
  (The houses are yours)

3ʳᵈ person singular: i tiji, e tija, të tijtë, të tijat

- a) I tiji is used with singular masculine noun - Libri është **i tiji**.
  (The book is his)
- b) e tija is used with singular feminine noun – Shtëpia është **e tija.**
  (The house is his)
- c) të tijtë is used with plural masculine noun – Librat janë **të tijtë.**
  (The books are his)
- d) të tijat is used with plural feminine noun - Shtëpitë janë **të tijat.**
  (The houses are his)

3rd person singular: i saji, e saja, të sajtë, të sajat

  a)   I saji is used with singular masculine noun - Libri është **i saji**.
       (The book is hers)
  b)   e saja is used with singular feminine noun – Shtëpia është **e saja.**
       (The house is hers)
  c)   të sajtë is used with plural masculine noun – Librat janë **të sajtë.**
       (The books are hers)
  d)   të sajat is used with plural feminine noun - Shtëpitë janë **të sajat.**
       (The houses are hers)

1st person plural: yni, jona, tanët, tonat

  a)   yni is used with singular masculine noun - Libri është **yni**.
       (The book is ours)
  b)   jona is used with singular feminine noun – Shtëpia është **jona.**
       (The house is ours)
  c)   të tanët is used with plural masculine noun – Librat janë **tanët.**
       (The books are ours)
  d)   të tonat is used with plural feminine noun - Shtëpitë janë **tonat.**
       (The houses are ours)

2nd person plural: juaji, juaja, tuajt, tuajat

  a)   juaji is used with singular masculine noun - Libri është **juaji**.
       (The book is yours)
  b)   juaja is used with singular feminine noun – Shtëpia është **juaja.**
       (The house is yours)
  c)   tuajt is used with plural masculine noun – Librat janë **tuajt.**
       (The books are yours)
  d)   tuajat is used with plural feminine noun - Shtëpitë janë **tuajat.**
       (The houses are yours)

3rd person plural (both feminine and masculine): i tyre, e tyre, të tyret, të tyret

a)   I tyre is used with singular masculine noun - Libri është **i tyri**.
     (The book is theirs)
b)   e tyre is used with singular feminine noun – Shtëpia është **e tyrja.**
     (The house is theirs)
c)   të tyre is used with plural masculine noun – Librat janë **të tyre.**
     (The books are theirs)
d)   të tyret is used with plural feminine noun - Shtëpitë janë **të tyret.**
     (The houses are theirs)

ADJECTIVES

Adjectives, just like nouns, have the grammatical categories of gender and number. In addition, they also have the grammatical category of degree. Some adjectives have the category of case as well (see Declension section below).

There are two types of adjectives:

1. Articulated adjectives (all adjectives preceded by an adjectival article):

i -for singular masculine adjectives: njeri **i** mirë (kind human), fëmijë **i** sjellshëm (polite child)

e- for feminine singular adjectives: grua **e** mirë (kind woman), vajzë **e** sjellshme (polite girl)

të - for plural masculine and feminine adjectives following <u>indefinite nouns</u>: njerëz **të** mirë (kind humans), fëmijë **të** sjellshëm (polite children), gra **të** mira (kind women), vajza **të** sjellshme (polite girls)

e - for plural masculine and feminine adjectives following <u>definite nouns</u>; njerëzit **e** mirë, fëmijët **e** sjellshëm, gratë **e** mira, vajzat **e** sjellshme.

The adjectival article, though separate, is an essential part of the adjective. The adjective cannot be used without it under no circumstances.

2. Unarticulated adjectives (they do not have an adjectival article, only the stem) – tërheqës (attractive), punëtor (hardworking), fatmirë (lucky), jetëgjatë (durable).

The position of adjectives

The adjective in Albanian almost always follows the noun:

vend **i pastër** (clean place),
Noun + Adjective

shtëpi **e madhe** (big house),
Noun + Adjective

Djalë **guximtar** (brave boy)
Noun + Adjective

However, the adjective may precede the noun when emphasizing or expressing strong emotions such as love, affection, surprise and so on:

i miri djalë (the kind boy, emotionally-charged)
Adjective + noun

e bukura vajzë (the beautiful girl, emotionally-charged)
Adjective + noun

Noun- Adjective Agreement

The form of the adjective is determined by the noun that precedes it (or in certain cases, as discussed above, the noun that follows it). The adjective agrees with the noun or pronoun it modifies in gender, number and case.

Baba **i mirë** (good father); nënë **e mirë** (good mother) – Gender agreement

("i mirë" changes to "e mirë" to agree with the feminine noun "mother")

Natë **e gjatë** (long night); net **të gjata** (long nights) – Number agreement

("e gjatë" changes to "të gjata" to agree with the plural feminine noun "net")

Hëna **e zbehtë** (the pale moon); hënës **së zbehtë** – Case agreement

("e zbehtë" changes to së zbehtë, that is the adjectival article from e to së changes in order to agree with the dative case of the noun "hënës")

Gender

There are feminine and masculine adjectives. An adjective has a different form when it defines a feminine noun and another form when it defines a masculine noun:

a)   Vend **i bukur** (beautiful place) – masculine noun "vend", masculine adj. "i bukur"
   Vajzë **e bukur** (beautiful girl) – feminine noun "vajzë", feminine adj. "e bukur"
b)   Burrë **vetmitar** (solitary man) – masculine noun "burrë", masculine adj. "vetmitar"
   Shtëpi **vetmitare** (solitary house) – feminine noun "shtëpi", feminine adj. "vetmitare"

As shown, the adjective always changes form to match the gender of the noun.

The representative gender of adjectives is the masculine. From the masculine form of the adjective, the feminine forms are derived. As there are two types of adjectives, articulated and non-articulated, there are two sets of rules.

Articulated adjectives form the feminine gender by:

1.   Changing the adjectival article from **i** to **e**:

provim **i vështirë** (hard exam)   –   detyrë **e vështirë** (hard task)
masculine N + masculine Adj.   Feminine N + feminine Adj.

2.   Changing the adjectival article from **i** to **e** plus taking the ending **-e**.

Oborr **i madh** (large yard)   –   shtëpi **e madhe** (large house)
masculine N + masculine Adj.   feminine N + feminine Adj.

Unarticulated adjectives, change the gender from masculine to feminine by:

1.   adding the ending - **e**

njeri **dinak** (cunning man)   –   dhelpër **dinake** (cunning fox)
masculine noun + masculine Adj.   feminine noun + feminine adj.

2.   By not changing the form:

Poet **gojëmjaltë** (honey-tongued poet) – poete **gojëmjaltë** (honey-tongued poetess)

Number

The adjectives in Albanian can be singular and plural depending on the number of the noun they accompany and their form changes accordingly.
In order to form the plural of adjectives, one has to take into the consideration two factors: 1) whether the adjective is masculine or feminine; 2) whether the adjective is articulated or unarticulated.

a)   An articulated masculine noun forms the plural by changing the singular adjectival article **i** to plural adjectival article **të**:

televizor **i** vjetër (old television)   –   televizorë **të** vjetër (old televisions)
singular masculine N + singular Adj.   plural masculine N + plural Adj.

b)   An unarticulated masculine noun forms the plural by adding **ë**:

nxënës punëtor (hardworking student)   –   nxënës punëtor**ë** (hardworking students)
singular masculine N + singular masculine Adj.   plural masculine N + plural masculine Adj.

c)   An articulated feminine noun forms the plural by changing **e** to **të**:

mbrëmje **e** këndshme (pleasant evening)   –   mbrëmje **të** këndshme (pleasant evenings)
singular feminine N + singular feminine Adj.   plural feminine N + plural feminine Adj.

d)   Most of the articulated feminine nouns, however, form the plural by changing
e to **të** and adding -**a**:

Ndërtesë **e lartë** (high building)
singular feminine N + singular feminine Adj

ndërtesa **të larta** (high buildings)
plural feminine N + plural feminine Adj.

e)   An unarticulated feminine noun does not change its form when used in plural:

Vajzë **lakmitare** (greedy girl)   –   vajza **lakmitare** (greedy girls)

All adjectives whose feminine singular form ends in -e have the same form for
the feminine plural. Additional examples are: shembullore (exemplary),
shqiptare (Albanian), popullore (popular), dinake (cunning) etc.

Declension

Adjectives are declined alongside nouns. In declension, articulated adjectives change only the adjectival article:

Masculine/ Singular   *Masculine/Plural*

Lisi **i gjatë** (the tall oak)   Lisat **e gjatë** (the tall oaks)
i,e/të/së lisit **të gjatë**   i,e/të/së lisave **të gjatë**
Lisit **të gjatë**   Lisave **të gjatë**
Lisin **e gjatë**   Lisat **e gjatë**
(prej) lisit **të gjatë**   (prej) lisave **të gjatë**

Feminine/Singular   *Feminine/Plural*

Shtëpia **e vjetër** (old house)   Shtëpitë **e vjetra** (old houses)
i,e/të/së shtëpisë **së vjetër**   i,e/të/së shtëpive **të vjetra**
Shtëpisë **së vjetër**   shtëpive **të vjetra**
Shtëpinë **e vjetër**   shtëpitë **e vjetra**
(prej) Shtëpisë **së vjetër**   (prej) shtëpive **të vjetra**

Note how the adjectival articles of the articulated adjectives in bold change form to agree with the case of the noun.

Unarticulated adjectives, on the other hand, when positioned as usual after the noun, do not undergo any change, therefore they do not decline:

Njeri **vetjak** (egoistic man)
I,e njeriut **vetjak**
Njeriut **vetjak**
Njeriun **vetjak**
Njeriut **vetjak**

Note how the unarticulated adjective "vetjak" does not change form in neither of the cases.

Degree

In Albanian, adjectives have three degrees:

1. Positive/Affirmative

2. Comparative

    a) Comparative degree of equality
    b Comparative degree of relative superiority
    c) Absolute Superlative degree
    d) Comparative degree of inferiority

3. Superlative

Positive Degree

Positive degree is the base form of the adjective that shows a quality or a characteristic of the referent, for example **i gjatë** (tall).

Comparative Degree

Comparative degree of equality is formed as below:

po aq (as) + adjective + sa (as)

Ai ishte	**po aq** i gjatë **sa**	i ati.
He was	as tall as	his father

Comparative degree of relative superiority is formed by adding the particle "më":

Më (more) + adjective + se/sesa (than)

("se" and "sesa" have the same meaning. Both can be used.)

Ai ishte   **më** i gjatë   **se/sesa**   i ati.
He was   taller   than   his father

Comparative degree of absolute superiority is formed by:

Më + adjective + i (masculine) / a (feminine)/ ët/it (plural masculine) / at (plural feminine)

Ai ishte   **më** i gjat**i**.
He was   the tallest.

Ajo ishte **më** e gjat**a**. (She was the tallest)
Djemtë tanë ishin **më** të gjat**ët**. (Our sons were the tallest.)
                  më të bukur**it.** (the most handsome)
Vajzat tona ishin **më** të gjat**at**. (Our daughters were the tallest).

Comparative degree of inferiority is formed by adding "më pak" which is equal to "less" in English:

Më pak + adjective + se/sesa

Ai ishte **më pak** i gjatë **sesa** i ati.

Superlative degree

Superlative degree is formed by adding adverbs before the adjectives. The most commonly used adverb is "shumë" (very).

Shumë i gjatë (very tall)
Shumë e sjellshme (very polite)
Shumë të këndshëm (very pleasant)
Shumë të dashura (very loving)

Other adverbs can also be used, such as mjaft (quite), tepër (too), fort (extremely, greatly), krejt (utterly), jashtëzakonisht (exceptionally), absolutisht (absolutely), tmerrësisht (terribly), çuditërisht (surprisingly), thellësisht (profoundly) etc.

VERBS

Verbs in Albanian are variable and take many different forms based on person, number, mood, tense and voice.

The verb ending is extremely important in Albanian because it denotes the voice, the mood, the tense, the person and the number.

- 35 -

THE VERB *TO BE*

Unë **jam** – I am

Ti **je** – You are

Ai **është** – He is

Ajo **është** – She is

Ne **jemi** – We are

Ju **jeni** – You are

Ata **janë** – They are (masculine)

Ato **janë** - They are (feminine)

Examples:

Unë **jam** shqiptare. (I am Albanian.)
Ti **je** 20 vjeç. – (You are 20 years old.)
Ajo **është** mësuese. – (She is a teacher.)
Ne **jemi** në punë. (We are at work.)
Ju **jeni** nga Anglia. (You are from England)
Ata **janë** njerëz të mirë. (They are good people.)

THE VERB *TO HAVE*

Unë **kam** – I have

Ti **ke** – You have

Ai **ka** – He has

Ajo **ka** – She has

Ne **kemi** – We have

Ju **keni** – You have

Ata **kanë** – They have (masculine)

Ato **kanë** – They have (feminine)

Examples:

Unë **kam** një shoqe të ngushtë. (I have a best friend.)
Ti **ke** sy të bukur. (You have beautiful eyes.)
Ai **ka** një makinë të shtrenjtë. (He has an expensive car.)
Ne **kemi** një motër të vogël. (We have a little sister.)
Ju **keni** ëndrra të mëdha. (You have big dreams.)
Ato **kanë** shumë rroba. (They have a lot of clothes.)

Person and number

The verb is used in three persons, 1st, 2nd and 3rd in singular and plural.
Just like the second person pronoun, the verb can be used in second person plural to refer to a single person when the speaker addresses people that he/she does not know in a polite manner or to maintain a degree of formality:

> (2nd person plural): **Dëshironi** një gotë me ujë, zotëri? – Would you like a glass of water, sir?
> (2nd person singular): **Dëshiron** një gotë me ujë, shoku im? – Do you want a glass of water, my friend?

The number of the verb is determined by the number of the subject. If the verb is in plural, that is because the subject is plural. It does not mean that there are multiple actions taking place.

> Ai **erdhi.** (He came.) – The verb is in third person singular to match the pronoun "he".
> Ata **erdhën.** (They came.) – The verb is in third person plural to match the pronoun "they".

The third person singular or plural may be used after collective nouns in the singular.

> 3rd person singular: Familja më **mbështet**. (My family supports me)
> 3rd person plural: Familja më **mbështesin**. (My family support me)

Voice

The verbs in Albanian can be in Active or Non-active voice. Non-active verb forms are mainly derived from active forms, however, some verbs do not have an active form.

Active

Non-active

laj (wash something)
mërzit (make someone upset)
(dress something/someone)

lahem (wash myself)
mërzitem (become upset)
vishem (get dressed)

Mood

There are six moods in Albanian:

1. Indicative (dëftore)
2. Subjunctive (lidhore)
3. Conditional (kushtore)
4. Admirative (habitore)
5. Optative (dëshirore)
6. Imperative (urdhërore)

These moods have specific verb forms in different persons and tenses (see conjugation below)

Tenses

In Albanian, there are 3 main tenses: Present, Past and Future.

a) The present simple
b) The past tense has five divisions:

1. Past Simple
2. Imperfect
3. Present Perfect
4. Past perfect
5. Pluperfect

c) The future tense in Albanian has two divisions:

1. Future Simple
2. Future Perfect

Conjugation

The Citation Form of a verb, the way it is represented in dictionaries, is first person, singular, active voice, indicative mood, present tense. The conjugation to which a verb belongs is determined by the ending of the Citation Form.

In Albanian, there are three types of conjugation:

1. 1ˢᵗ Conjugation - verbs have a Citation Form ending in a vowel + j or more specifically ending in **-oj, -aj, -ej, ëj -ij, -uj, -yj**: kënd**oj** (sing), lu**aj** (play), kërc**ej** (dance), b**ëj** (do), v**ij** (come), h**yj** (enter)

2. 2ⁿᵈ Conjugation – verbs have a Citation Form ending in a consonant other than – j: qe**sh** (laugh), pye**s** (ask), përdo**r** (use), sho**h** (see), ha**p** (open), da**l** (go out)

3. 3ʳᵈ Conjugation – verbs have a Citation Form ending in a vowel: h**a** (eat), p**i** (drink), fl**e** (sleep), d**i** (know), du**a** (want), z**ë** (catch), l**ë** (leave)

Since the verbs are used in Active and Non-active voice, there is also conjugation of active verbs and conjugation of Non-active verbs.

Conjugation of Verbs in Indicative Mood

The indicative mood in Albanian is the most commonly used. The action denoted by the verb in the indicative mood is possible; the statement is presented as fact. It is the only mood that has all the tenses in Albanian, 8 in total.

Present Simple

Present Simple denotes an action that is a habit, that happens regularly or on a repeated manner.

Person	1st conjugation		2nd conjugation		3rd conjugation	
	Active (think)	Non-active (become)	Active (ask)	Non-active (lean on/rely on)	Active (drink)	Non-active (to be put/ to be placed)
Unë	mendo**j**	bë**hem**	pyes	mbështet**em**	pi	vi**hem**
Ti	mendo**n**	bë**hesh**	pyet	mbështet**esh**	pi	vi**hesh**
Ai/Ajo	mendo**n**	bë**het**	pyet	mbështet**et**	pi	vi**het**
Ne	mendo**jmë**	Bë**hemi**	pyes**im**	mbështet**emi**	pi**më**	vi**hemi**
Ju	mendo**ni**	bë**heni**	pyes**ni**	mbështet**eni**	pini	vi**heni**
Ata/Ato	mendo**jnë**	bë**hen**	pyes**in**	mbështet**en**	pi**në**	vi**hen**

How about present continuous?

In Albanian, the particle "po" or the verb to be (jam) + gerund added to the verb, is equal to the present progressive in English and denotes an action that is happening at the moment of speaking:

a) Present Continuous with particle "po"

Po mendoj. – I am thinking.
Po vihem në pozitë të vështirë – I am being put in a difficult position. (Non-active)

b) Present Continuous with the verb to be (jam) + gerund

Jam duke pyetur. – I am asking.
Jam duke qeshur. – I am laughing.

Past simple

Past Simple denotes actions completed in the past that have no connection with the present.

Person	1st conjugation		2nd conjugation		3rd conjugation	
	Active (thought)	Non-active (became)	Active (asked)	Non-active (leaned on/ relied on)	Active (drank)	Non-active (was put/ was placed)
Unë	mendo**va**	u bëra	Pye**ta**	u mbështeta	pi**va**	u vura
Ti	mendo**ve**	u bëre	Pye**te**	u mbështete	pi**ve**	u vure
Ai/Ajo	mendo**i**	u bë	Pye**ti**	u mbështet	pi**u**	u vu
Ne	Mend**uam**	u bëmë	Pyet**ëm**	u mbështetëm	pi**më**	u vumë
Ju	Mend**uat**	u bëtë	Pyet**ët**	u mbështetët	pi**të**	u vutë
Ata/Ato	Mend**uan**	u bënë	Pyet**ën**	u mbështetën	pi**në**	u vunë

Imperfect

Imperfect tense is used to denote habits of the past, repeated actions in the past that went on up until a particular time in the past. It is also used to give background information such as describing the setting, the characters, the atmosphere and so on.

Person	1st conjugation		2nd conjugation		3rd conjugation	
	Active (thought/ used to think)	Non-active (used to become)	Active (used to ask)	Non-active (used to lean on on/rely on)	Active (used to drink)	Non-Active (used to be put/ placed)
Unë	mendo**ja**	bë**hesha**	pye**sja**	mbështet**esha**	pi**ja**	vi**hesha**
Ti	mendo**je**	bë**heshe**	pye**sje**	mbështet**eshe**	pi**je**	vi**heshe**
Ai/Ajo	mend**onte**	bë**hej**	pye**ste**	mbështet**ej**	pi**nte**	vi**hej**
Ne	mendo**nim**	bë**heshim**	pye**snim**	mbështet**eshim**	pi**nim**	vi**heshim**
Ju	mendo**nit**	bë**heshit**	pye**snit**	mbështet**eshit**	pi**nit**	vi**heshit**
Ata/Ato	mendo**nin**	bë**heshin**	pye**snin**	mbështet**eshin**	pi**nin**	vi**heshin**

What about past continuous?

Similar to present continuous, if the particle "po" or the construction "isha duke + verb" is added to a verb in the imperfect tense, the new construction is equivalent to past continuous in English and denotes an action that was in progress in the past for some time.

a) Po mendoja - I was thinking.
    Po luaja. – I was playing.

b) Isha duke pyetur. – I was asking.
    Isha duke qeshur. – I was laughing.

Present Perfect

It is a compound tense that is formed by the present tense of the auxiliary verb kam (have) + pjesorja (past participle). The Non-active is formed by jam (be) + past participle. It denotes an action that was completed in the past but has a connection with the present.

Note how only the verb kam and jam change. The conjugation is the same for all verbs.

Person	1st conjugation		2nd conjugation		3rd conjugation	
	Active Have thought	Non-active have become	Active Have asked	Non-active (have leaned on on/ relied on)	Active have drunk	Non-active have been put/ placed
Unë	kam menduar	jam bërë	kam pyetur	jam mbështetur	kam pirë	jam vënë
Ti	ke menduar	je bërë	ke pyetur	je mbështetur	ke pirë	je vënë
Ai/Ajo	ka menduar	është bërë	ka pyetur	është mbështetur	ka pirë	është vënë

Ne	kemi menduar	jemi bërë	kemi pyetur	jemi mbështetur	kemi pirë	jemi vënë
Ju	keni menduar	jeni bërë	keni pyetur	jeni mbështetur	keni pirë	jeni vënë
Ata/Ato	kanë menduar	janë bërë	kanë pyetur	janë mbështetur	kanë pirë	janë vënë

Pluperfect

It denotes an action that began in the past and was completed before another action in the past. It is equivalent to the past perfect English tense.

Pluperfect is a compound tense. It is formed by:

Active - Kisha (the verb to have in past tense) + main verb in past participle

Non-active- Isha (the verb to be in past tense) + main verb in past participle

Note how only the verb kisha and isha change. The conjugation is the same for all verbs.

Person	1st conjugation		2nd conjugation		3rd conjugation	
	Active Had thought	Non-active had become	Active Had asked	Non-active (had leaned on on/ relied on)	Active had drunk	Non-active had been put / placed
Unë	kisha menduar	isha bërë	kisha pyetur	isha mbështetur	kisha pirë	isha vënë
Ti	kishe menduar	ishe bërë	kishe pyetur	ishe mbështetur	kishe pirë	ishe vënë
Ai/ Ajo	kishte menduar	ishte bërë	kishte pyetur	ishte mbështetur	kishte pirë	ishte vënë
Ne	kishim menduar	ishim bërë	kishim pyetur	ishim mbështetur	kishim pirë	ishim vënë
Ju	kishit menduar	ishit bërë	kishit pyetur	ishit mbështetur	kishit pirë	ishit vënë
Ata/ Ato	kishin menduar	ishin bërë	kishin pyetur	ishin mbështetur	kishin pirë	ishin vënë

Past Perfect

Its usage is similar to pluperfect, it denotes an action completed before another action or before a definite time in the past.

It is a compound tense. It is formed by:

Active- Pata (the verb to have in imperfect tense) + main verb in past participle
Non-active - Qeshë (the verb to be in imperfect tense) + main verb in past participle

Note how only the verb pata changes. The conjugation is the same for all verbs.

Person	1st conjugation		2nd conjugation		3rd conjugation	
	Active Had thought	Non-active Had become	Active Had asked	Non-active (had leaned on on/relied on)	Active Had drunk	Non-active Had been put/placed
Unë	pata menduar	qeshë bërë	pata pyetur	qeshë mbështetur	pata pirë	qeshë vënë
Ti	pate menduar	qe bërë	pate pyetur	qe mbështetur	pate pirë	qe vënë
Ai/Ajo	pat menduar	qe bërë	pat pyetur	qe mbështetur	pat pirë	qe vënë
Ne	patëm menduar	qemë bërë	patëm pyetur	qemë mbështetur	patëm pirë	qemë vënë
Ju	patët menduar	qetë bërë	patët pyetur	qetë mbështetur	patët pirë	qetë vënë
Ata/Ato	patën menduar	qenë bërë	patën pyetur	qenë mbështetur	patën pirë	qenë vënë

Future Simple

It denotes an action that is expected to be completed at some time in the future. It is formed by:

Particle "do" + main verb in subjunctive mood "të + verb". Ex. do + të luaj (verb in subjunctive mood)

"Do të" in Albanian is equal to "will" and "be going to" in English.

Person	1st conjugation		2nd con-jugation	3rd conjugation	
	Active Will think	Non-active Will become	Active Will ask	Active Will drink	Non-active Will be put/ placed
Unë	do të mendoj	do të bëhem	do të pyes	do të pi	do të vihem
Ti	do të mendosh	do të bëhesh	do të pyesësh	do të pish	do të vihesh
Ai/Ajo	do të mendojë	do të bëhet	do të pyesë	do të pijë	do të vihet
Ne	do të mendojmë	do të bëhemi	do të pyesim	do të pimë	do të vihemi
Ju	do të mendoni	do të bëheni	do të pyesni	do të pini	do të viheni
Ata/Ato	do të mendojnë	do të bëhen	do të pyesin	do të pinë	do të vihen

Future Perfect

It denotes an action that will be completed in the future before another action or a definite time in the future. It can also be used to express possible actions in the past. It is a compound tense. It is formed by:

The verb kam (to have) in future tense +   verb in past participle

do të kem   + menduar (I will have thought)

"Do të kem" is equal to "will have" in English.

Person	1st conjugation		2nd conjugation		3rd conjugation	
	Active Will have thought	Non-active Will have become	Active Will have asked	Non-active (will have leaned on on/relied on)	Active will have drunk	Non-active will have been put/ placed
Unë	do të kem menduar	do të jem bërë	do të kem pyetur	do të jem mbështetur	do të kem pirë	do të jem vënë
Ti	do të kesh menduar	do të jesh bërë	do të kesh pyetur	do të jesh mbështetur	do të kesh pirë	do të jesh vënë
Ai/Ajo	do të ketë menduar	do të jetë bërë	do të ketë pyetur	do të jetë mbështetur	do të ketë pirë	do të jetë vënë
Ne	do të kemi menduar	do të jemi bërë	do të kemi pyetur	do të jemi mbështetur	do të kemi pirë	do të jemi vënë
Ju	do të keni menduar	do të jeni bërë	do të keni pyetur	do të jeni mbështetur	do të keni pirë	do të jeni vënë
Ata/Ato	do të kenë menduar	do të jenë bërë	do të kenë pyetur	do të jenë mbështetur	do të kenë pirë	do të jenë vënë

Conjugation of Verbs in Subjunctive mood

Subjunctive mood is characterized by the particle "të" which precedes all verb forms. It is equivalent to the "to-infinitive" in English. Subjunctive mood is used after modal verbs such as mundem (can), mund (may), duhet (must), dua, dëshiroj (want), preferoj (prefer), kam nevojë (need).

Subjunctive mood has four tenses: present tense, imperfect, present perfect and pluperfect.

Present Tense

The present tense of indicative mood denotes an action that is possible, desirable, obligatory or indispensable:

Mund **të studiojmë** bashkë. (We can study together) – Possible action

Dëshiroj **të mësoj** shqip. (I want to learn Albanian.) – Desirable

Duhet **të jem** në punë në orën tetë. (I must be at work at eight o'clock) – Obligatory

Duhet të mësoj patjetër për këtë provim. (I absolutely must study for this exam) – Indispensable

Person	1st conjugation		2nd conjugation		3rd conjugation	
	Active (to think)	Non-active (to become)	Active (to ask)	Non-active (to lean on /rely on)	Active (to drink)	Non-active (to be put/ placed)
Unë	të mendoj	të bëhem	të pyes	të mbështetem	të pi	të vihem
Ti	të mendosh	të bëhesh	të pyesësh	të mbështetesh	të pish	të vihesh
Ai/Ajo	të mendojë	të bëhet	të pyesë	të mbështetet	të pijë	të vihet
Ne	të mendo-jmë	të bëhemi	të pyesim	të mbështetemi	të pimë	të vihemi
Ju	të mendoni	të bëheni	të pyesni	të mbështeteni	të pini	të viheni
Ata/ Ato	të mendojnë	të bëhen	të pyesin	të mbështeten	të pinë	të vihen

Imperfect

The imperfect of subjunctive mood denotes an action that either had to be completed or could have been completed in the past.

Unë duhej të flisja me të. (I had to talk to him) – Had to be completed.
Unë mund të flisja me të. (I could have talked to him) – could have been completed

Person	1st conjugation		2nd conjugation		3rd conjugation	
	Active (to think)	Non-active (to become)	Active (to ask)	Non-active (to lean on/ rely on)	Active (to drink)	Non-active (to be put/ placed)
Unë	të mendoja	të bëhesha	të pyesja	të mbështetesha	të pija	të vihesha
Ti	të mendoje	të bëheshe	të pyesje	të mbështeteshe	të pije	të viheshe
Ai/Ajo	të mendonte	të bëhej	të pyeste	të mbështetej	të pinte	të vihej
Ne	të mendon-im	të ëheshim	të py-esnim	të mbështeteshim	të pinim	të viheshim
Ju	të mendonit	të bëheshit	të pyesnit	të mbështeteshit	të pinit	të viheshit
Ata/ Ato	të mendonin	të bëheshin	të pyesnin	të mbështeteshin	të pinin	të viheshin

Present perfect

Denotes an action that could have been completed before the moment of speaking.

Ti mund të kesh menduar se kam harruar. (You could have thought I have forgot.)

Person	1st conjugation		2nd conjugation		3rd conjugation	
	Active (to have thought)	Non -active (to have become)	Active (to have asked)	Non-active (to have leaned on/relied on)	Active (to have drunk)	Non-active (to have been put/placed)
Unë	të kem menduar	të jem bërë	të kem pyetur	të jem mbështetur	të kem pirë	të jem vënë

Ti	të kesh menduar	të jesh bërë	të kesh pyetur	të jesh mbështetur	Të kesh pirë	të jesh vënë
Ai/Ajo	të ketë menduar	të jetë bërë	të ketë pyetur	të jetë mbështetur	të ketë pirë	të jetë vënë
Ne	të kemi menduar	të jemi bërë	të kemi pyetur	të jemi mbështetur	të kemi pirë	të jemi vënë
Ju	të keni menduar	të jeni bërë	të keni pyetur	të jeni mbështetur	të keni pirë	të jeni vënë
Ata/Ato	të kenë menduar	të jenë bërë	të kenë pyetur	të jenë mbështetur	të kenë pirë	të jenë vënë

Pluperfect

Denotes an action that could have been completed before another action in the past.

Unë duhej të kisha pyetur se ku ishe. (I should have asked where you were).

Person	1st conjugation		2nd conjugation		3rd conjugation	
	Active	Non-active	Active	Non-active	Active	Non-active
Unë	të kisha menduar	të isha bërë	të kisha pyetur	të isha mbështetur	të kisha pirë	të isha vënë
Ti	të kishe menduar	të ishe bërë	të kishe pyetur	të ishe mbështetur	të kishe pirë	të ishe vënë
Ai/Ajo	të kishte menduar	të ishte bërë	të kishte pyetur	të ishte mbështetur	të kishte pirë	të ishte vënë
Ne	të kishim menduar	të ishim bërë	të kishim pyetur	të ishim mbështetur	të kishim pirë	të ishim vënë
Ju	të kishit menduar	të ishit bërë	të kishit pyetur	të ishit mbështetur	të kishit pirë	të ishit vënë
Ata/Ato	të kishin menduar	të ishin bërë	të kishin pyetur	të ishin mbështetur	të kishin pirë	të ishin vënë

Conjugation of Verbs in Conditional Mood

The verb in conditional mood denotes an action that is possible provided another condition is fulfilled. Conditional mood has two tenses: present tense and present perfect.

Present Tense

It denotes that an action in the present would be possible if a condition were to be fulfilled.
Ex. Po ta dija, do të tregoja. (If I knew it, I would tell it).

Since the speaker does not know something, he/she cannot tell it.

Person	1st conjugation		2nd conjugation		3rd conjugation	
	Active (would think)	Non-active (would become)	Active (would ask)	Non-active (would lean on/ rely on)	Active (would drink)	Non-active (would be put/placed)
Unë	do të mendoja	do të bëhesha	do të pyesja	do të bështetesha	do të pija	do të vihesha
Ti	do të mendoje	do të bëheshe	do të pyesje	do të mbështeteshe	do të pije	do të viheshe
Ai/Ajo	do të mendonte	do të bëhej	do të pyeste	do të mbështetej	do të pinte	do të vihej
Ne	do të mendonim	do të bëheshim	do të pyesnim	do të mbështeteshim	do të pinim	do të viheshim
Ju	do të mendonit	do të bëheshit	do të pyesnit	do të mbështeteshit	do të pinit	do të viheshit
Ata/Ato	do të mendonin	do të bëheshin	do të pyesnin	do të mbështeteshin	do të pinin	do të viheshin

Present Perfect

It denotes an action that would have been completed in the past if a condition in the past had been fulfilled. Since the condition has not been fulfilled, the action is unrealized:

Po të mësonim, do ta kishim kaluar provimin.
(If we had studied, we would have passed the test.)

Since the condition of studying has not been fulfilled, the exam has not been passed, therefore passing the exam is unrealized.

Person	1st conjugation		2nd conjugation		3rd conjugation	
	Active (would have thought)	Non-active (would have become)	Active (would have asked)	Non-active (would have leaned on/ relied on)	Active (would have drunk)	Non-active (would have been put/ placed)
Unë	do të kisha menduar	Do të isha bërë	do të kisha pyetur	do të isha mbështetur	do të kisha pirë	do të isha vënë
Ti	do të kishe menduar	do të ishe bërë	do të kishe pyetur	do të ishe mbështetur	do të kishe pirë	do të ishe vënë
Ai/Ajo	do të kishte menduar	do të ishte bërë	do të kishte pyetur	do të ishte mbështetur	do të kishte pirë	do të ishte vënë
Ne	do të kishim menduar	do të ishim bërë	do të kishim pyetur	do të ishim mbështetur	do të kishim pirë	do të ishim vënë
Ju	do të kishit menduar	do të ishit bërë	do të kishit pyetur	do të ishit mbështetur	do të kishit pirë	do të ishit vënë
Ata/Ato	do të kishin menduar	do të ishin bërë	do të kishin pyetur	do të ishin mbështetur	do të kishin pirë	do të ishin vënë

Conjugation of verbs in the Admirative Mood

The verb in the admirative mood expresses an action that is unexpected and causes surprise, or disbelief. It can also be used for emphasis.

Ua, ai **këndoka** bukur - Wow, he sings beautifully.

Sa rrjedhshëm **fliskeni** shqip!- How fluently you speak Albanian!

Sa me zë të lartë që **qeshkan**. - How loudly they laugh.

Sa lehtë **u bëkan** këto biskota. – How easy these cookies are made. (Non-active)

Po unë dikam shumë gjëra për Shqipërinë - So I know a lot of things about Albania (surprising oneself).

Admirative mood does not exist in English. It has four tenses: present, imperfect, present perfect and pluperfect. Imperfect and pluperfect are rarely used.

Present Simple

Denotes an action that happens at the moment of speaking and surprises the speaker. It is formed by adding the endings **-kam, -ke, -ka, -kemi, -keni, -kan** to the stem of the verb.

Person	1st conjugation		2nd conjugation		3rd conjugation	
	Active	Non-active	Active	Non-active	Active	Non-active
Unë	mendokam	u bëkam	pyeskam	u mbështetkam	pikam	u vënkam
Ti	mendoke	u bëke	pyeske	u mbështetke	pike	u vënke
Ai/Ajo	mendoka	u bëka	pyeska	u mbështetka	pika	u vënka
Ne	mendokcmi	u bëkemi	pyeskemi	u mbështetkemi	pikemi	u vënkemi
Ju	mendokeni	u bëkeni	pyeskeni	u mbështetkeni	pikeni	u vënkeni
Ata/Ato	mendokan	u bëkan	pyeskan	u mbështetkan	pikan	u vënkan

Imperfect

Denotes an action that went on during a certain point in the past and caused surprise, doubt or disagreement.

Sa shumë pyeskëshit! – You ask a lot of questions! (with a tone of annoyance)
Sa mirë luakësh! – How well he played!

It is formed by adding the endings **-kësha, -këshe, -kësh, -këshim, -këshit, -këshin** to the stem of the verb.

Person	1st conjugation		2nd conjugation		3rd conjugation	
	Active	Non-active	Active	Non-active	Active	Non-active
Unë	mendokësha	u bëkësha	pyeskësha	u mbështetkësha	pikësha	u vënkësha
Ti	mendokëshe	u bëkëshe	pyeskëshe	u mbështetkëshe	pikëshe	u vënkëshe
Ai/Ajo	mendokësh	u bëkësh	pyeskësh	u mbështetkësh	pikësh	u vënkësh
Ne	mendokëshim	u bëkëshim	pyeskëshim	u mbështetkëshim	pikëshim	u vënkëshim
Ju	mendokëshit	u bëkëshit	pyeskëshit	u mbështetkëshit	pikëshit	u vënkëshit
Ata/Ato	mendokëshin	u bëkëshin	pyeskëshin	u mbështetkëshin	pikëshin	u vënkëshin

Present Perfect

Denotes an action that is already completed but the speaker expresses surprise, disbelief or disagreement in the present.

Sa gjatë paskam folur! – How long I have spoken!
Sa shumë njerëz që paskan ardhur! – How many people have come!

Paskam and qenkam change in different persons.

Person	1st conjugation		2nd conjugation		3rd conjugation	
	Active	Non-active	Active	Non-active	Active	Non-active
Unë	Paskam menduar	qenkam bërë	Paskam pyetur	qenkam mbështetur	Paskam pirë	qenkam vënë
Ti	Paske menduar	qenke bërë	Paske pyetur	qenke mbështetur	Paske pirë	qenke vënë
Ai/Ajo	Paska menduar	qenka bërë	Paska pyetur	qenka mbështetur	Paska pirë	qenka vënë
Ne	Paskemi menduar	qenkemi bërë	Paskemi pyetur	qenkemi mbështetur	Paskemi pirë	qenkemi vënë
Ju	Paskeni menduar	qenkeni bërë	Paskeni pyetur	qenkeni mbështetur	Paskeni pirë	qenkeni vënë
Ata/Ato	Paskan menduar	qenkan bërë	Paskan pyetur	qenkan mbështetur	Paskan pirë	qenkan vënë

Pluperfect

Denotes an action that happened in the past before another action in the past and expresses the speaker's surprise, doubt or disagreement:

Ju paskëshit menduar se unë nuk ia dal dot. – You had thought I cannot make it. (in disbelief)
Ajo paskësh pritur që ta ftonim. – She had expected to be invited. (surprised)
Ata paskëshin folur me të pra. – Well, they had talked to her then. (doubt)

Paskësha and qenkësha change through different persons.

Person	1st conjugation		2nd conjugation		3rd conjugation	
	Active	Non-active	Active	Non-active	Active	Non-active
Unë	Paskësha menduar	qenkësha bërë	Paskësha pyetur	qenkësha mbështetur	Paskësha pirë	qenkësha vënë
Ti	Paskëshe menduar	qenkëshe bërë	Paskëshe pyetur	qenkëshe mbështetur	Paskëshe pirë	qenkëshe vënë
Ai/Ajo	Paskësh menduar	qenkësh bërë	Paskësh pyetur	qenkësh mbështetur	Paskësh pirë	qenkësh vënë
Ne	Paskëshim menduar	qenkëshim bërë	Paskëshim pyetur	qenkëshim mbështetur	Paskëshim pirë	qenkëshim vënë
Ju	Paskëshit menduar	qenkëshit bërë	Paskëshit pyetur	qenkëshit mbështetur	Paskëshit pirë	qenkëshit vënë
Ata/Ato	Paskëshin menduar	qenkëshin bërë	Paskëshin pyetur	qenkëshan mbështetur	Paskëshin pirë	qenkëshin vënë

Conjugation of verbs in Optative Mood

The verb in optative mood expresses the action as a wish or a curse.

Optative mood has two tenses: present and present perfect.

Present Simple

Expresses the wish or the curse of the speaker either for the moment of speaking or after the moment of speaking.

Mendofsh mirë për hapin e radhës. – May you think well of your next step (as a wish).
Jetofshin gjatë. – May they live long (wish)
Shkofsh e mos u kthefsh – May you go and never return. (as a curse)
U bëfsh 100 vjeç. – May you live to be a hundred. (Non-active)

Person	1st conjugation		2nd conjugation		3rd conjugation	
	Active	Non-active	Active	Non-active	Active	Non-active
Unë	mendofsha	u bëfsha	pyetsha	u mbështetsha	pifsha	u vënça
Ti	mendofsh	u bëfsh	pyetsh	u mbështetsh	pifsh	u vënç
Ai/Ajo	mendoftë	u bëftë	pyettë	u mbështettë	piftë	u vëntë
Ne	mendofshim	u bëfshim	pyetshim	u mbështetshim	pifshim	u vënçim
Ju	mendofshi	u bëfshi	pyetshi	u mbështetshi	pifshi	u vënçi
Ata/Ato	mendofshin	u bëfshin	pyetshin	u mbështetshin	pifshin	u vënçin

Present Perfect

It is rarely used. It expresses a wish or a curse made for a certain point in time in the past.

Na pastë marrë të ligat! (May they have taken the evils away from us)
Paçim punuar mirë (May we have done a good work).

Person	1st conjugation		2nd conjugation		3rd conjugation	
	Active	Non-active	Active	Non-active	Active	Non-active
Unë	paça menduar	qofsha bërë	paça pyetur	qofsha mbështetur	paça pirë	qofsha vënë
Ti	paç menduar	qofsh bërë	paç pyetur	qofsh mbështetur	paç pirë	qofsh vënë
Ai/Ajo	pastë menduar	qoftë bërë	pastë pyetur	qoftë mbështetur	Pastë pirë	qoftë vënë
Ne	paçim menduar	qofshim bërë	paçim pyetur	qofshim mbështetur	paçim pirë	qofshim vënë
Ju	paçi menduar	qofshi bërë	paçi pyetur	qofshi mbështetur	paçi pirë	qofshi vënë
Ata/Ato	paçin menduar	qofshin bërë	paçin pyetur	qofshin mbështetur	paçin pirë	qofshin vënë

The Conjugation of Verbs in Imperative Mood

The verb in imperative expresses an action in the form of an order, advice or request.

Shko shpejt! – Go quickly! (order)

Ulu me mua të lutem. – Sit with me please. (request)

Flisni me të. – Talk to him. (advice)

Imperative mood has only one tense: present. It also has only one person: 2nd person singular and plural.

Person	1st conjugation		2nd conjugation		3rd conjugation	
	Active	Non-active	Active	Non-active	Active	Non-active
Ti	Mendo	bëhu	Pyet	mbështetu	Pi	Vihu
Ju	Mendoni	bëhuni	Pyesni	mbështetuni	Pini	Vihuni

The second person plural in imperative is the same as the second person plural in the indicative mood.

There is also the form with the ending – më such as:

Shkruamë – write to me

Duamë -love me.

Thuamë – tell me.

Negation particles

In order to form the negative of the verb, the particles "nuk" and "s'" are used. They have the same meaning and function and are always placed before the verb.

Flas – I speak
Nuk flas/ **S'**flas – I don't speak

Only modal verbs and abbreviated forms can come between the negation particle and the verb.

S'**mund** të flas – I cannot talk (modal verb)
Nuk **më** flet dot – He cannot talk to me at all. (abbreviated form)

Another particle to form the negative of verbs is "mos" which is used in:
Subjunctive mood: mos të di (not to know), mos të flas (not to talk)
Imperative mood: mos fol (don't talk), mos eja (don't come)
Optative mood: mos qofsha (not to be), mos ardhsha (not to come) – as a wish
Infinitive – për të mos punuar (not to work)
Gerund – duke mos folur (not talking)

The particle "pa" is also used with the past participle to form the negative infinitive and it has the meaning "without".

Iku **pa thënë** gjë. – He left without saying anything.

WORD ORDER

In Albanian, word order is relatively free; words can take different positions within the sentence without changing their syntactic function. Considering that in Albanian, the grammatical function of words is indicated by corresponding endings rather than by their position, their syntactic function is clear regardless of their place within the sentence. However, one still needs to be careful that the words are arranged in such a manner that they match the syntactic nature of Albanian and that they sound natural. The defining rules of the word order relate, first and foremost, to the way the subject, predicate and object are arranged.

> Djali i ndihmoi vajzës. (The boy helped the girl)
> Vajzës i ndihmoi djali. (The girl was helped by the boy)

In the examples above, it is clear that, in both sentences, even though they change position, "djali" is a subject and "vajzës" an indirect object because of their endings **-i** and **-s**.

For the most part, whether in spoken or written Albanian, the most common word order is: Subject (S)– Predicate (P):

Muzika u ndal. (The music stopped)
Ajo foli bukur. (She spoke beautifully)

However, to bring the action to the fore or for matters of style or emotional expression, the reverse order is used:

U ndal muzika.
Foli bukur ajo.

The same applies to the direct object (DO), complements (C) and adverbials (Adv.):

Mësuesi e shpjegoi **detyrën**. (The teacher explained the task) (S + P + O)
Detyrën e shpjegoi mësuesi. (DO + P + S)

Ajo është **mësuese**. (She is a teacher) (S + P + SC)
Mësuese është ajo. (SC + P + S)

Mbërritëm në shkollë **herët**. (We arrived to school early) (S + Adv. of place + Adv. of time)
Herët mbërritëm në shkollë. (Adv. of time + P + Adv. of place)

The sentences are still grammatically and semantically correct even when the order is reversed.

Apart from its most common position in the beginning of the sentence, the subject can also be used in the middle and at the end of the sentence. To illustrate:

1. Erdhën vonë ata. (Erdhën -came, vonë-late, ata-they. The subject is positioned at the end of the sentence.)
2. Fëmijët ne i pamë nga larg. (Fëmijët – children, ne – we, pamë – see, nga larg – from afar. The subject is positioned in the middle of the sentence)

The adverbial phrases in Albanian do not have a fixed position. They can move freely within the sentences from the beginning to the middle and to the end of the sentences. Even so, they are typically placed after the verb on which they depend.

Mbrëmja erdhi **shpejt.** (The evening came fast)
Ai u zgjua **në orën pesë.** (He woke up at five)

But the opposite is equally possible:

Shpejt erdhi mbrëmja.
Në orën pesë u zgjua.

Another interesting aspect is that the order of words within a sentence can also be determined by the way information is conveyed. Typically, the first part of the sentence will contain the information that is already known, followed by the information that is new or unknown. Let's clarify it through an example:

Blerimi i bleu ushqimet.
Blerim bought the food.

In the sentence above, Blerimi- subject is the known information, the listeners/readers know who Blerim is, whereas "i bleu ushqimet" is the new information, something that was not known before. In Albanian, this is the common word order, where the unknown information follows the known information. The opposite is also possible. Hence, it can be concluded that the word order in a sentence depends, on one hand, on the grammatical characteristics of the language, and on the other hand, on what we want to convey and how we want to convey it.

In Albanian, it is possible to form sentences without its most important constituents such as subject and predicate when they are implied by the context or for stylistic reasons.

Natë. (Night.) -Can be used in fiction for stylistic reasons.
Hynë brenda pa bërë zhurmë. (Went inside without making any noise). This sentence does not have a subject. The verb "hynë" agrees with third person plural and the reader/listener will know from the context who the sentence is referring to.

The word order in questions

Usually, in questions that begin with one of the question words such as: Ku? (Where?), Kur? (When?), Sa? (How much?) Si? (How?) Pse (Why?) and so on, the question word (QW) is followed by the predicate (P), and then the predicate is followed by the subject (S) or other sentence elements, as shown in the examples below:

1. Ku u takuat ju të dy? (Where did you two meet?) (QW + P + S)
2. Kur filloi mësimi?   (When did the lesson start?) (QW + P + S)

3. Sa i bleve këto këpucë? (How much did you pay for these shoes?) (QW + P + DO)

4. Si e bëre këtë ushtrim? (How did you do this exercise?) (QW + P + SO)

5. Pse e telefonove kaq vonë? (Why did you call him so late?) (QW + P + Adv.)

It is one of the cases when the word order in Albanian is fixed. It is not natural to say for example: Kur mësimi filloi? **X**; Si këtë ushtrim e bëre? **X**

www.ingramcontent.com/pod-product-compliance
Lightning Source LLC
Chambersburg PA
CBHW040200160726
48006CB00014B/1839